SEDAN

The Ford Sedan is the family car which fully meets every requirement of comfort, convenience, service and economy. Its use is always a source of keen enjoyment. Women appreciate the ease with which it is driven, the safety which it affords.

With finer upholstery, adjustable window regulators, and many refinements in chassis construction, The Ford Sedan is an even greater value than ever. And the price has never before been so low.

List your order now. Avoid disappointment. A small down payment—the balance on easy terms, or you may take advantage of the

Ford Weekly Purchase Plan

which makes it still easier for you to own a Ford.

$645

F.O.B. DETROIT

Comfort and Convenience

for
Social
Professional
and Business
Uses —

$530
F.O.B. DETROIT

Ford
THE UNIVERSAL CAR
SEDAN

$595 F.O.B. DETROIT

MODEL T

HOW HENRY FORD BUILT A LEGEND

DAVID WEITZMAN

CROWN PUBLISHERS ♛ NEW YORK

"I will build a motor car for the great multitude. It will be large enough for the family, but small enough for the individual to run and care for. It will be constructed of the best materials, by the best men to be hired, after the simplest designs modern engineering can devise. . . . But it will be so low in price that no man making a good salary will be unable to own one—and enjoy with his family the blessing of hours of pleasure in God's great open spaces."

—Henry Ford

1910 Model T roadster with rear bucket seat.

Henry Ford's Quadracycle, 1896, owed much of its technology to the bicycle—wire wheels, steel-tube frame, and chain-and-sprocket drive. It had a two-cylinder engine and the steering was by tiller, at the end of which was a button connected to a doorbell to warn pedestrians.

HENRY FORD

grew up on a farm in Michigan but often neglected his chores to tinker with the farm machinery. "Chicken is for hawks," he said, "milk is a mess." So he left the farm to become an apprentice in a shop that repaired steam engines. He learned to fix watches, clocks, waterwheels, and turbines. By age seventeen, he qualified as a journeyman machinist. And by his early thirties, when he built the Quadracycle, Ford knew firsthand much of what he needed to make his car for the people. He had been gathering all the pieces of the puzzle, and when he had every piece in place, it made a Model T.

The motorcar had been around for a while when Ford got down to work. But cars at that time were built by craftsmen, one individually shaped piece at a time, and could be afforded only by the very rich. They werc big, heavy cars that might go all of five miles per hour on a good road, none of which could be found in rural America. The wisdom of the day said that only big, expensive cars were profitable. But Ford sensed a restlessness in the American spirit: "Everybody wants to be someplace he ain't. And as soon as he gets there, he wants to go right back." He believed that if he could make a car that was rugged and dependable and inexpensive, everyone would buy one.

Americans like Eli Whitney, Samuel Colt, and Cyrus McCormick had all pioneered ways to manufacture things more quickly, precisely, and cheaply many years earlier, and Ford put their ideas to brilliant use in making the Model T.

His first innovation was to make the car using interchangeable parts. Once Ford and his engineers had established a prototype car, they "froze" the model and set about making large quantities of its many parts.

The second innovation was to break the job of putting the car together into very basic tasks, and to assign each task to a different worker. That way no one worker had to know how to put together an entire car, which eliminated the need for highly skilled, and highly paid, craftsmen. Ford's workers only needed to do one small piece of the job—and they needed to do it over and over again, all day long.

◀ About 250 women are on the Ford payroll, hired to do "women's work"—cutting and sewing fabrics in the upholstery department and assembling small parts needing a woman's "delicate touch," as with these workers who are assembling the magnets for the magneto.

Many Ford workers are recent immigrants—Italians, Armenians, Russians, Syrians, Germans, Hungarians, Romanians, Serbians, Croatians, Greeks, Czechs, Lithuanians, Poles—most of whom speak not a word of English when they start work.

"It's push and hustle and go. The man behind may shove his work along to you at any moment—you must not hold him back; at any moment the man in front may be ready for another piece to work on—he must not be kept waiting."
—Paolo Consiglio, assembly-line worker

▶ An example of the work slide. Assembly of the flywheel magneto, which generates electricity for the car, begins with the closest worker and is moved back through the line. Bins of interchangeable parts are close to hand.

Once the components of a car had been assembled, these pieces were brought together and a team of workers built a single car from start to finish. This "stationary assembly" of a car took 12 hours, 28 minutes.

This was the fastest a car had ever been put together, but for Ford it was too slow. Workers in the other parts of the plant were mass-producing thousands of parts each workday. Parts began to pile up faster than they could be used.

"The cars were assembled on the spot. They would bring the chassis and the motor and body to one place. I would say there would be ten or fifteen spots for assembling. The body, as near as I could remember, was brought on a hand truck. The fellows could lift a car body easy enough. After they were assembled, they were driven out."
—*Karel Skrivanek, assembly-line worker*

The first Model T's are fitted with wooden wheels just like wagon wheels, which are crafted in the traditional way by wheelwrights.

Model T chassis are made of super strong, super light vanadium steel. And they are assembled using a new three-point suspension that can withstand the bumpiest of roads. These advances make the Model T sturdier than other cars and also peppier, as its engine needs to propel less weight.

Ford and his engineers decided to use the assembly-line technique to build the entire car.

The difference was astonishing. Workers on the first moving line could assemble a complete chassis in only 2 hours, 40 minutes—nearly *ten* hours less than it took to assemble the car in one spot.

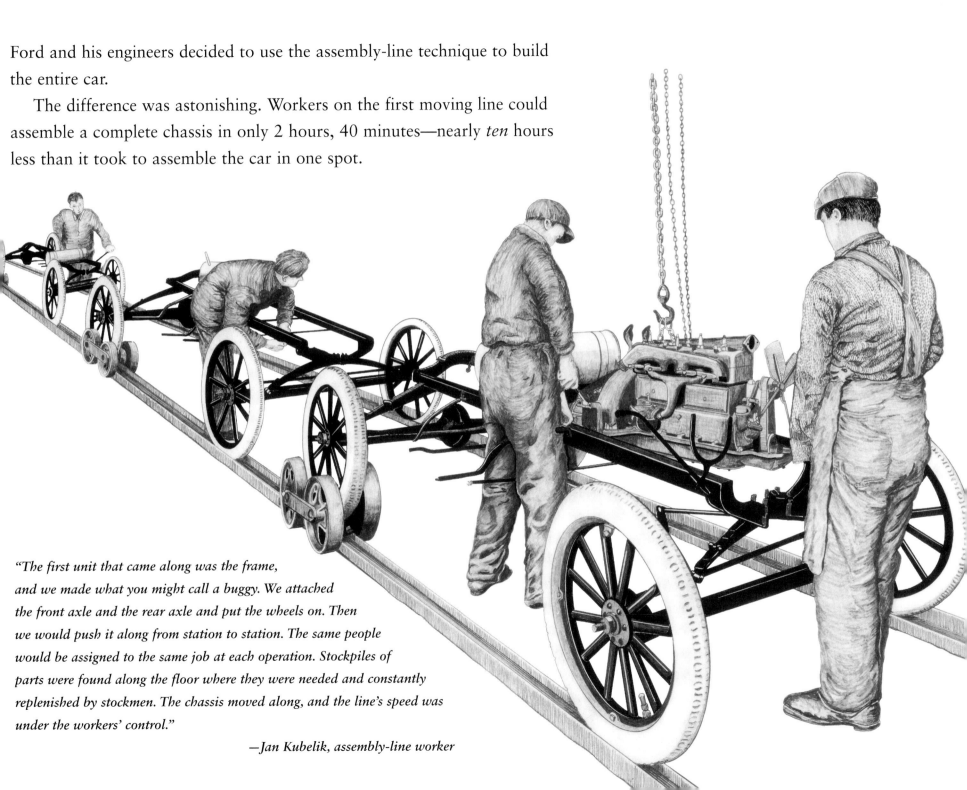

"The first unit that came along was the frame, and we made what you might call a buggy. We attached the front axle and the rear axle and put the wheels on. Then we would push it along from station to station. The same people would be assigned to the same job at each operation. Stockpiles of parts were found along the floor where they were needed and constantly replenished by stockmen. The chassis moved along, and the line's speed was under the workers' control."

—*Jan Kubelik, assembly-line worker*

Even with such success, Ford and his team felt they could go faster. Their next step was to place the car on a conveyor, which moved the chassis along at a fixed rate—72 inches a minute. Workers had to perform their functions quickly before the car rolled away.

Ford engineers also experimented with the best height for work. When they raised the entire conveyor line, workers didn't have to stoop, which increased their comfort and, more importantly, their efficiency. On April 30, 1914, assembly-line workers built 1,212 chassis in one eight-hour day. The time to complete each chassis had been cut to just 1 hour and 33 minutes.

◀ At first, stockmen carry parts to the lines, but later conveyors do their job. This man is supplying the line workers with mufflers.

Ford line workers are strictly forbidden to speak to one another. There can be no distractions on the line.

▶ Lines are built at two different heights, 24 1/2 inches for shorter men and 26 3/4 inches for taller workers.

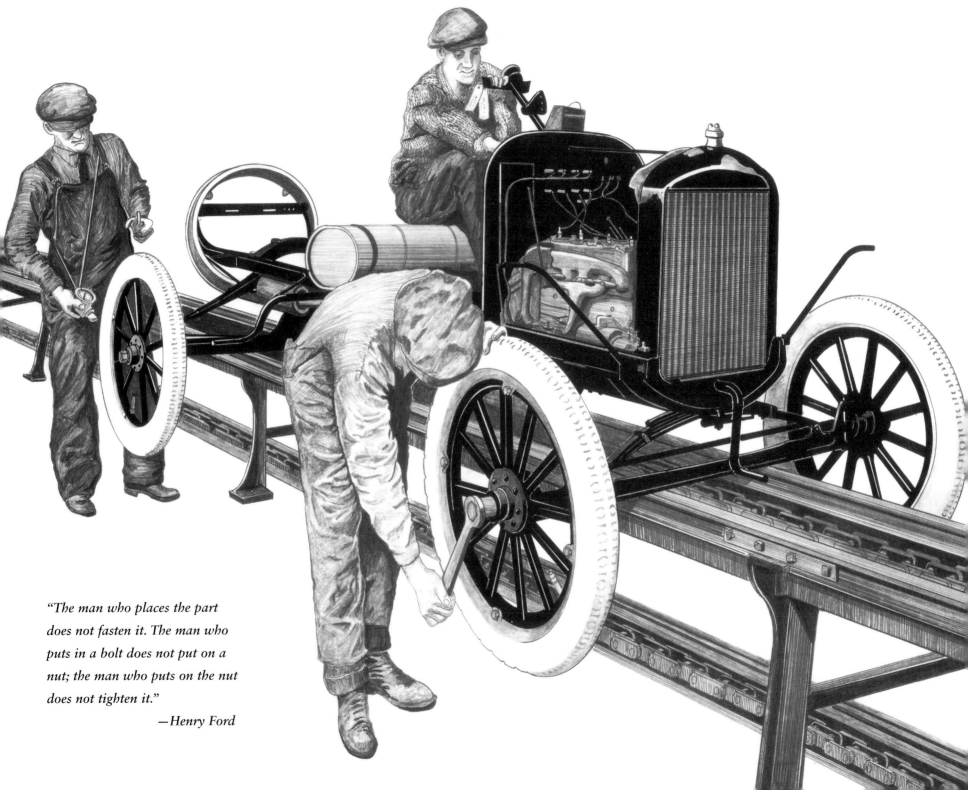

"The man who places the part does not fasten it. The man who puts in a bolt does not put on a nut; the man who puts on the nut does not tighten it."

—Henry Ford

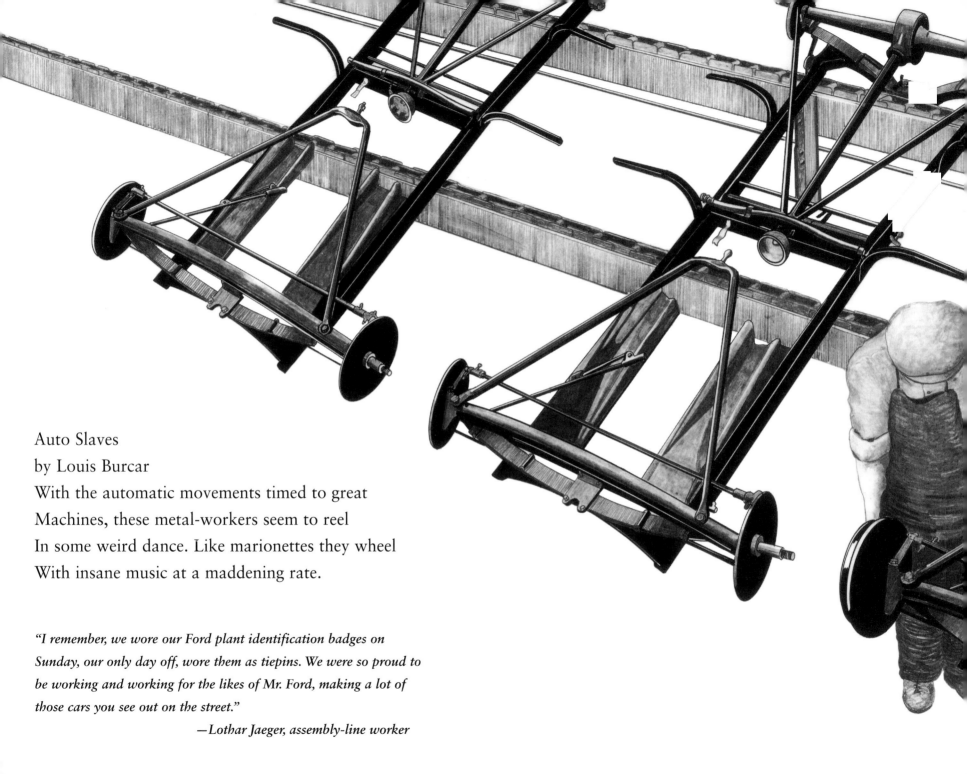

Auto Slaves
by Louis Burcar
With the automatic movements timed to great
Machines, these metal-workers seem to reel
In some weird dance. Like marionettes they wheel
With insane music at a maddening rate.

"*I remember, we wore our Ford plant identification badges on
Sunday, our only day off, wore them as tiepins. We were so proud to
be working and working for the likes of Mr. Ford, making a lot of
those cars you see out on the street.*"
—*Lothar Jaeger, assembly-line worker*

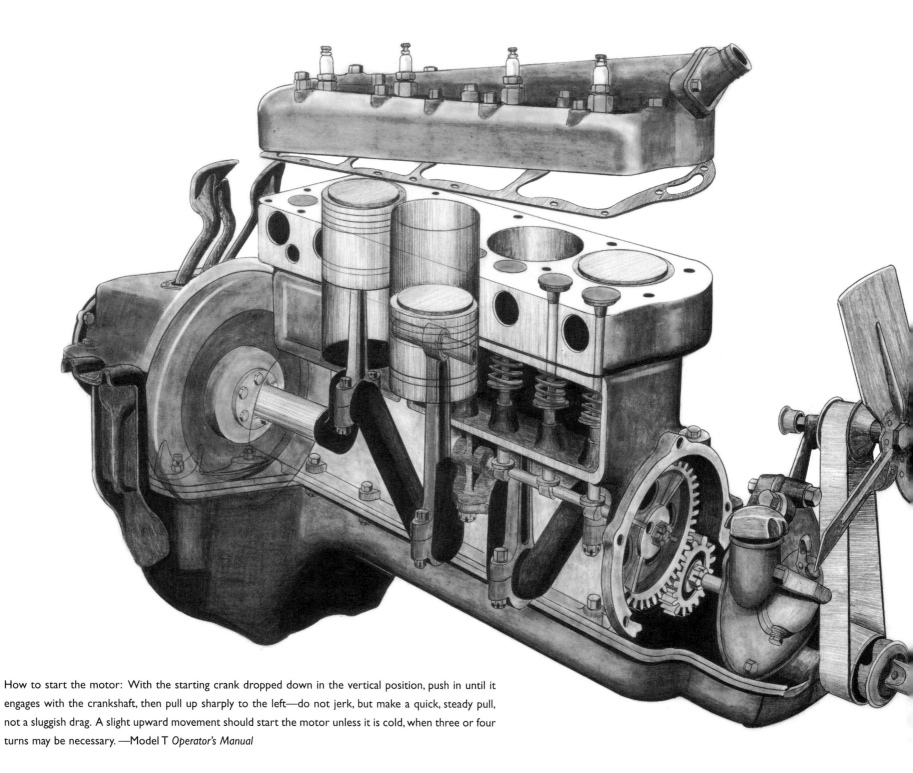

How to start the motor: With the starting crank dropped down in the vertical position, push in until it engages with the crankshaft, then pull up sharply to the left—do not jerk, but make a quick, steady pull, not a sluggish drag. A slight upward movement should start the motor unless it is cold, when three or four turns may be necessary. —Model T *Operator's Manual*

Ford Model T Engine

- 4-cylinder/4-cycle, water-cooled
- 3 ³⁄₄" bore x 4" stroke
- 20 horsepower, 2 speeds forward/1 reverse
- 35–40 miles per hour, 18–20 miles per gallon
- 400 pounds with transmission

Ford's new car also had an innovative new engine. Existing engines needed constant maintenance—most required the driver to stop and add oil every few miles! They had individually cast cylinders that were bolted to a crankcase (like motorcycle engines). Henry Ford asked his engineers to come up with a way to cast the cylinders and crankcase all in one piece to make manufacture and maintenance easier. And so the modern internal combustion engine was born.

▼ Engines are attached to an electric motor for "burning in." Because new engines are tight, the electric motor has to work hard at first to turn an engine. An ammeter shows how many amps the motor is drawing, so the operator can easily tell when the engine is burned in—the motor draws fewer amps.

▶ Engine blocks are made by pouring molten iron into precise molds. This worker is placing cores into the mold, which will form the complicated openings inside the block. When the casting has cooled, a worker will break out the cores.

▼ These men easily handle a ladle that holds 1,250 pounds of molten iron. Foundrymen pour 1,300 engine blocks a day.

Henry Ford employs more African Americans than any other manufacturer.

At first, engines were built like the cars, one at a time at stationary workbenches. It took one man almost ten hours to assemble one engine. Then an observer using a stopwatch discovered that workers spent about four hours—almost half the workday—walking back and forth. On a moving assembly line, with the work brought to the man, it took only about four hours to complete an engine.

◄ Ford engineers develop specialized machine tools to make the work go faster. This machine drills 24 holes at once from three directions. An operator simply positions the engine block, then pulls a starting lever. The machine completes the operation, and the man removes the block and positions the next piece.

Michigan was the center of the nation's carriage and wagon industry. Now those skilled workers applied their trade to a new machine. The body of a car required extensive handwork and was created much like a fine piece of furniture. Each car received two primer coats and two varnish coats of paint and was then hand-rubbed with pumice and water for a mirror finish.

The frames were originally covered with a thin wood skin, but from about 1911 on, they are covered with stamped steel panels.

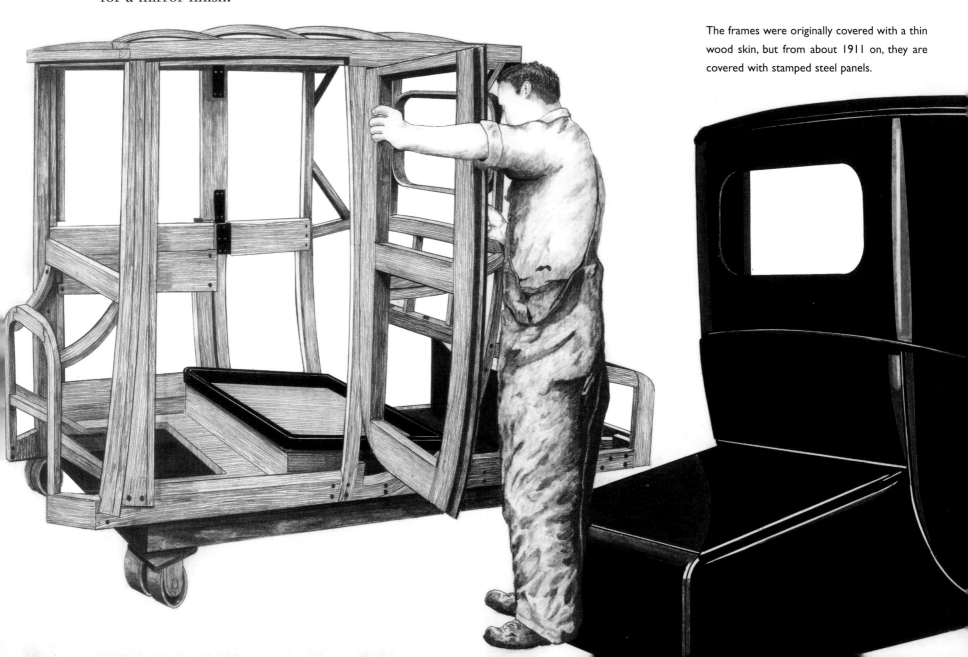

▲ The bodies, too, move along a conveyor as they are painted, upholstered, trimmed out, and fitted with tops. Upholsterers stuff horsehair into the leather seat covers sewn by women workers.

▼ Paint is flowed on. The extra runs off into the trough and returns to the paint tank. One gallon covers 11 bodies.

Each year 380 acres of glass are used for the Model T windows and 400,000 hides are used for the seats.

Moving along at six feet a minute, the nearly completed chassis slid off the rails to run, for the first time, on its own wheels. As the final inspector tagged any defects, a worker tightened the nut holding the handwheel to the steering shaft, and another filled the radiator with water. After 41 separate operations, the chassis was at last complete.

▲ Operation 41: Tighten two bolts holding the front-axle radius rod to the frame.

► The chassis comes off the line and onto friction wheels set into the floor for a running test. The driver cranks the motor to life, adjusts the engine speed, throws the control lever forward, and motors out the door. The auto is mobile at last!

Finally, chassis and body came together to make a complete car. The body chute eliminated all the lifting and carrying of the early days. An endless belt (controlled by the lever man at the upper right) brought painted and upholstered bodies to the top of the chute. Midway down the chute, ropes connected to a gallows frame were attached to the body. When the frame was swung forward, the body dropped neatly onto a waiting chassis.

A short drive then brought the shiny Model T's to a shipping platform and long lines of waiting boxcars.

"Any Model T owner can change his touring car into a roadster. One chassis, two bodies, and a buyer has a car for all seasons."

—*Ford Times*

▶ The ropes have just been released from a body dropped onto a chassis. The man on the box will raise the gallows frame upright so the two men at the lower end of the chute can attach the ropes to the next body.

Ford's Highland Park plant, designed by architect Albert Kahn, is one of the first industrial buildings constructed with reinforced concrete, making it possible to have unobstructed work areas (perfect for the new assembly lines) and 50,000 square feet of windows and sky-lights. The gleaming glass factory is known as the Crystal Palace.

The finished cars—so recently assembled!—were then disassembled for shipping across the country. The body, chassis, wheels, and a wooden barrel of small parts for each car were tagged to make sure they got to the same destination.

The bodies are lifted off the chassis, the wheels are removed, and the chassis are stacked on end, seven in a row—///////—in each boxcar.

In the first year of production, Ford built about 10,000 Model T's and the price was $850. (In 1908, a schoolteacher earned about $500 per year.) As the improvements being made on the assembly line worked their magic, production nearly doubled every couple years and the price plummeted. In 1915, more than 300,000 Model T's were built and the price had dropped to $490. By 1923, Ford reached an all-time production high of more than 2,000,000 Model T's, with the cheapest model selling for just $265.

In 1900, there were 500 cars in New York State. Just ten years later the number had grown to 62,660. In that same time the number of cars in California had grown from 780 to 44,120.

1916 is the first year automobile production exceeds buggy production.

The Ford is the only car
For service near and far.
—Ford advertising slogan

The first automobile dealers were either in the horse-and-wagon trade or bicycle dealers. These men also became the first driving teachers. The Ford Company sent out mechanics to teach them how to repair and maintain the Model T. As advertised, the car could be completely disassembled and repaired with the tool kit that came with it: pliers, a screwdriver, and an adjustable wrench. By 1912, just four years after the first Model T was introduced, there were over 7,000 Ford dealers around the country. That meant a dealer in almost every town of 2,000 people or more.

The Model T was a huge success—Americans were in love! The automobile ended the isolation of rural families, just as Ford had intended. As one farm woman explained when asked why her family had bought a car before they had indoor plumbing, "Why, you can't go to town in a bathtub."

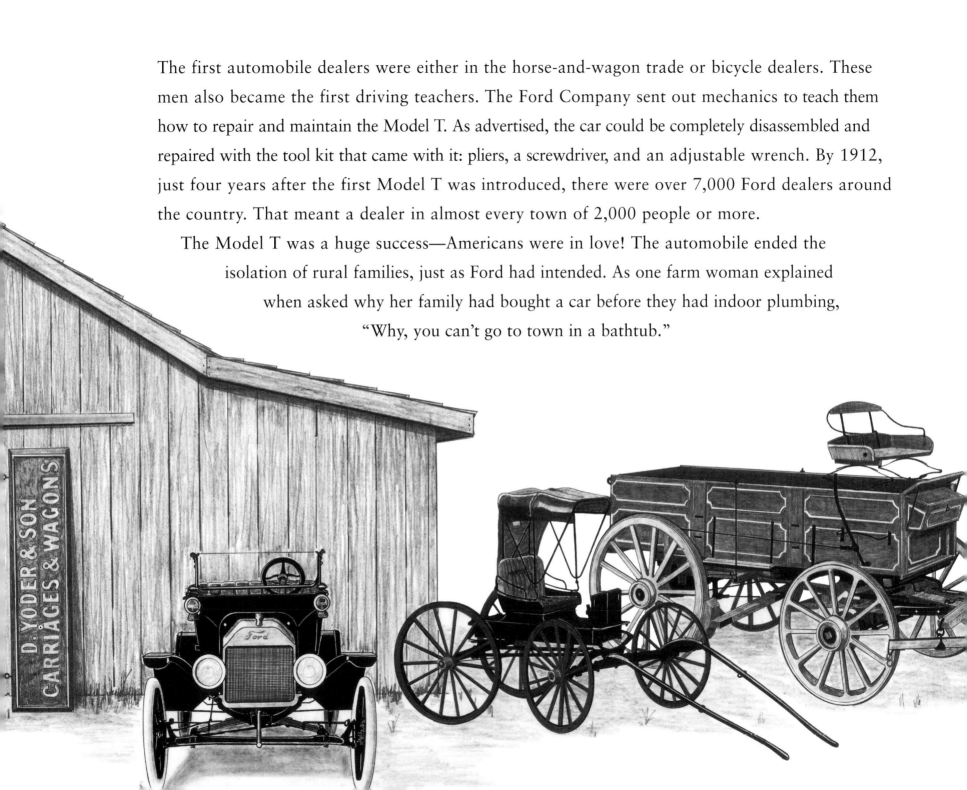

Whole new industries sprang up because of the popular Model T. Suddenly there was a great demand for gasoline, and so people went to work both refining it and selling it. At first, motorists bought gasoline at the general store (not unlike the little convenience stores that sell gas today). It was sold in glass bottles with funnel-shaped tops or simply by the bucketful. But soon there were full-service "filling stations." Attendants pumped gas, cleaned your windshield, and checked engine oil, the water level in the radiator, and tire pressure. Massive quantities of rubber would be needed to make those tires. Roads were being paved and bridges built, and soon there would be the beginnings of the interstate highway system.

The Model T changed the automobile from a toy for the wealthy to a tough, hardworking, and fun transport for the people. A new Model T rolled off the assembly line every 45 seconds for years and years. All told, Ford would produce more than 15 million of his car for the masses.

And America would never be the same again.

Filling station, Winchester, Kentucky, 1914.

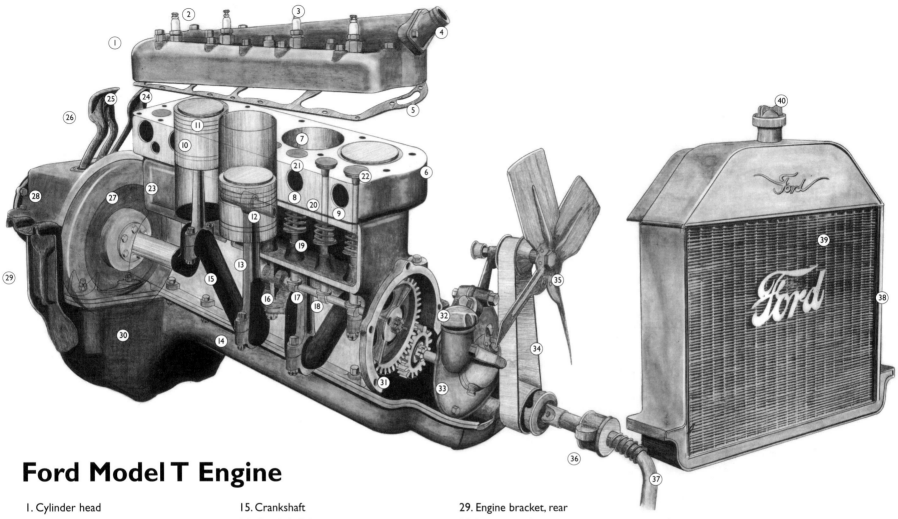

Ford Model T Engine

1. Cylinder head
2. Cylinder-cap screws
3. Spark plugs
4. Cylinder-head outlet (to radiator)
5. Head gasket
6. Engine block
7. Combustion chamber
8. Intake port
9. Exhaust port
10. Piston
11. Piston ring
12. Piston pin
13. Connecting rod
14. Rod bearing

15. Crankshaft
16. Crankshaft bearing, center
17. Camshaft
18. Cam
19. Valve spring
20. Push rod
21. Intake valve
22. Exhaust valve
23. Valve cover
24. High and slow speed pedal
25. Reverse pedal
26. Brake pedal
27. Flywheel
28. Transmission case

29. Engine bracket, rear
30. Lower crankcase
31. Timing gears
32. Oil filler cap
33. Cylinder cover, front
34. Fan belt
35. Fan
36. Engine bracket, front
37. Starting crank
38. Radiator
39. Radiator tubes and fins
40. Radiator filler cap

For Louis Nathan Weitzman.

The best dad a boy could have.

1914 Model T touring car.

For all their help, my thanks to the staff of the Henry Ford Museum's Historical Resources Research Center, especially Linda Skolarus, Manager of Reference Services, and Robert Casey, Curator of Transportation.

Special thanks also to Stephen Hubert of the Model T Ford Club International for the use of Model T advertising from his personal collection.

Copyright © 2002 by David Weitzman

All rights reserved under International and Pan-American Copyright Conventions. No part of this book may be reproduced or transmitted in any form or by any means, electronic or mechanical, including photocopying, recording, or by any information storage and retrieval system, without permission in writing from the publisher. Published by Crown Publishers, a division of Random House, Inc., 1540 Broadway, New York, New York 10036. CROWN and colophon are trademarks of Random House, Inc.

www.randomhouse.com/kids

Library of Congress Cataloging-in-Publication Data
Weitzman, David.
Model T : how Henry Ford built a legend / written & illustrated by David Weitzman.
p. cm.
Summary: A detailed look at the creation of Henry Ford's Model T automobile, including its assembly-line production.
ISBN 0-375-81107-9 (trade) — ISBN 0-375-91107-3 (lib. bdg.)
1. Ford Model T automobile—Juvenile literature. 2. Assembly-line methods—Juvenile literature. 3. Ford Motor Company—Juvenile literature.
4. Ford, Henry, 1863–1947—Juvenile literature. [1. Ford Model T automobile. 2. Automobiles—History. 3. Ford, Henry, 1863–1947.] I. Title.
TL215.F7 W45 2002   629.222'2—dc21   2001053931

Printed in the United States of America
July 2002

10 9 8 7 6 5 4 3 2 1   First Edition

Ford — THE UNIVERSAL CAR

$348.00 F.O.B. DETROIT

Never Before a Value Like This

Ford SEDAN

An Even Greater Value

Important Improvements

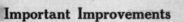

The great Ford Organization never ceases in its efforts to make better, more efficient and longer lived the Ford products which are even now so satisfactorily serving their owners. Here are a few of the most recent improvements to Ford Cars.

Pistons have been made ¾ lb. lighter and matched accurately for weight.

Reciprocating parts made lighter and accurately balanced. This reduces vibration, insures longer life to motor, quicker pick-up and more miles per gallon.

All bearings polished on crankshaft reduces friction and makes for easier running and long life bearings.

Improved wiring absolutely protects wires

BE closer to church, to school, to business, to your friends, to the pleasures of the world. Be independent of distance and conditions. Have safe, economical, dependable transportation.

Decide today—*right now*—to buy *your* Ford Touring car. The extremely low price at which it is sold — the lowest in the history of the Ford Motor Company

$298
F.O.B. DETROIT

The New One-Man Top and Slanting Wind-Shield

Another improvement to the Ford Touring Car, an improvement which adds greatly to the appearance of the car—an improvement which gives every advantage and convenience of this well-known type of top and windshield construction.

And at an astonishingly low price. Think of it!

— A Better Car for Less Money

than the Ford Runabout—there isn't a car made that gives so much for so little money.

The Ford Runabout is serving men, merchants and manufacturers in every line. It is saving them time—doubling sales and increasing earnings. It will do as much for you or your business.

Let us give you the proofs and explain our easy payment plan. Come in, write or phone.

$269
F.O.B. DETROIT